Animal Habitats

Written by Margaret MacDonald

Picture Dictionary

Amazon rainforest

Great Barrier Reef

Arctic islands

Everglades

Sahara desert

Animals live in many places on Earth.
Some animals live on land.
Some animals live in water.

This cheetah lives on grasslands in Africa.

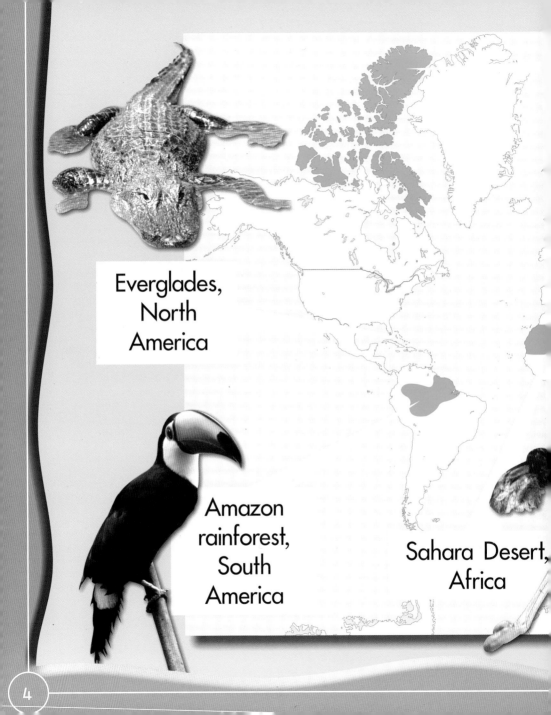

Everglades,
North
America

Amazon
rainforest,
South
America

Sahara Desert,
Africa

Arctic islands

Great Barrier Reef,
Australia

Great Barrier Reef

Some animals live
in the water
near the Great Barrier Reef.
They find their food
near the reef.
They hide from enemies
in the reef.

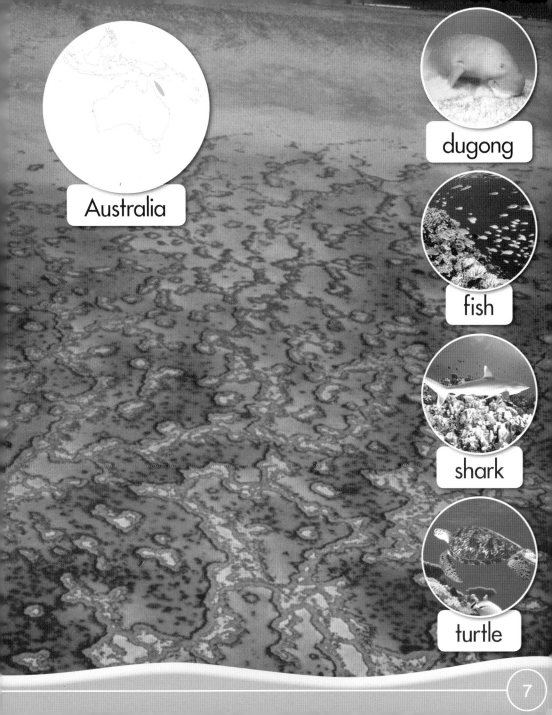

Australia

dugong

fish

shark

turtle

Everglades

Some animals live
in the swampy Everglades.
They find their food there.
They hide from enemies there.
Some animals live in the water.
Some live on the land.
Some live in the water
and on the land.

North America

alligator

egret

flamingo

lizard

Amazon Rainforest

It is hot and wet
in the Amazon rainforest.
Some animals live
in the rainforest trees.
They find food in the trees.
They hide from enemies
in the trees.
Some animals live
on the forest floor.
They find food
on the forest floor.

South America

anaconda

monkey

sloth

toucan

Sahara Desert

It is hot and dry
in the Sahara Desert.
Desert animals have to keep cool.
They have to find water.
Some animals live underground.
They hide from the sun.
Some animals get water
from the food they eat.

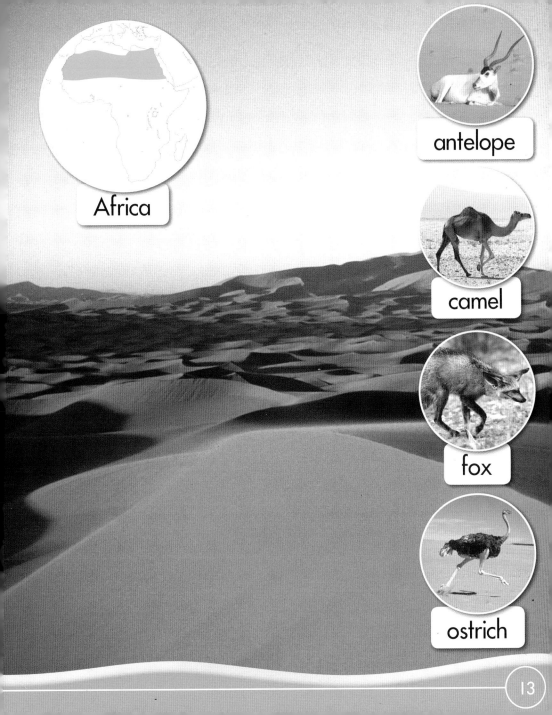

Africa

antelope

camel

fox

ostrich

Arctic Islands

Some animals live
on the Arctic islands.
It is very cold
on the Arctic islands.
There is snow and ice all year.
The animals have thick skin
and fur to keep them warm.

Arctic islands

Arctic hare

polar bear

seal

walrus

1. Choose an animal in the book.

2. Find out more about it.

3. Find out what it eats.

4. Find out who its enemies are.

5. Find out what its home is like.

6. Draw a picture of your animal in its home.

Do you know the dictionary words?